# THIS BOOK

# BELONGS TO :

- - - - - - - - - - - - - - - - - - - - - - - - - - - - - -

- - - - - - - - - - - - - - - - - - - - - - - - - - - - - -

- - - - - - - - - - - - - - - - - - - - - - - - - - - - - -

# HOW TO DRAW

# HOW TO DRAW

# HOW TO DRAW

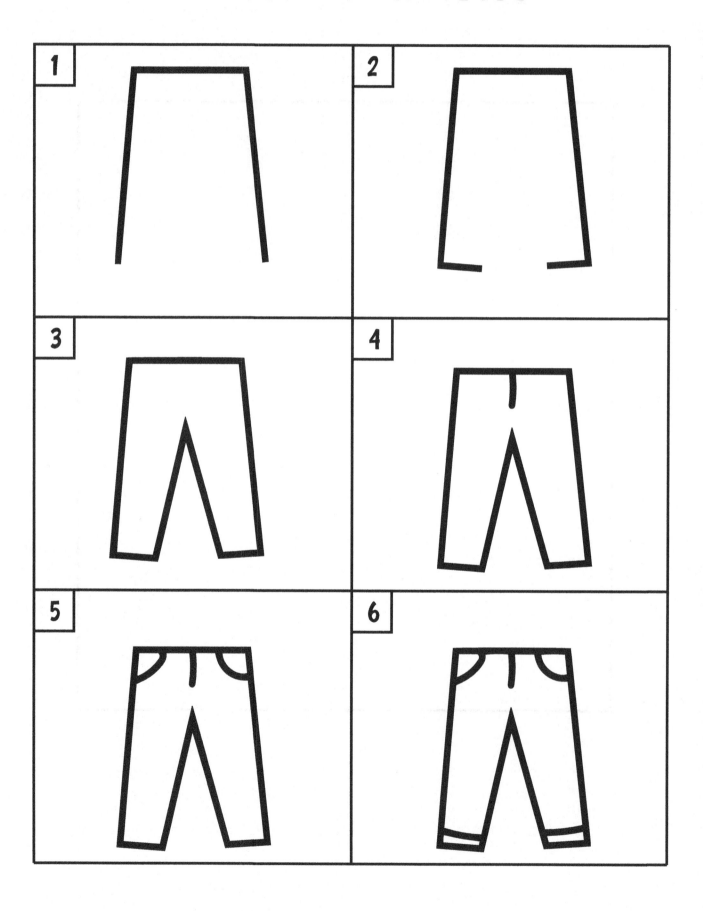

# HOW TO DRAW

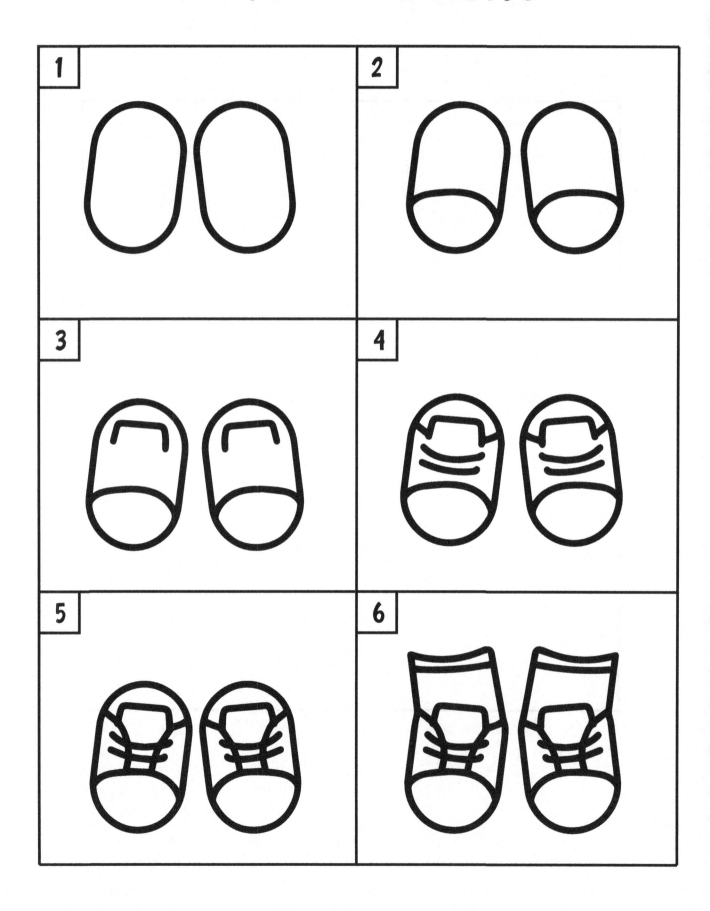

# HOW TO DRAW

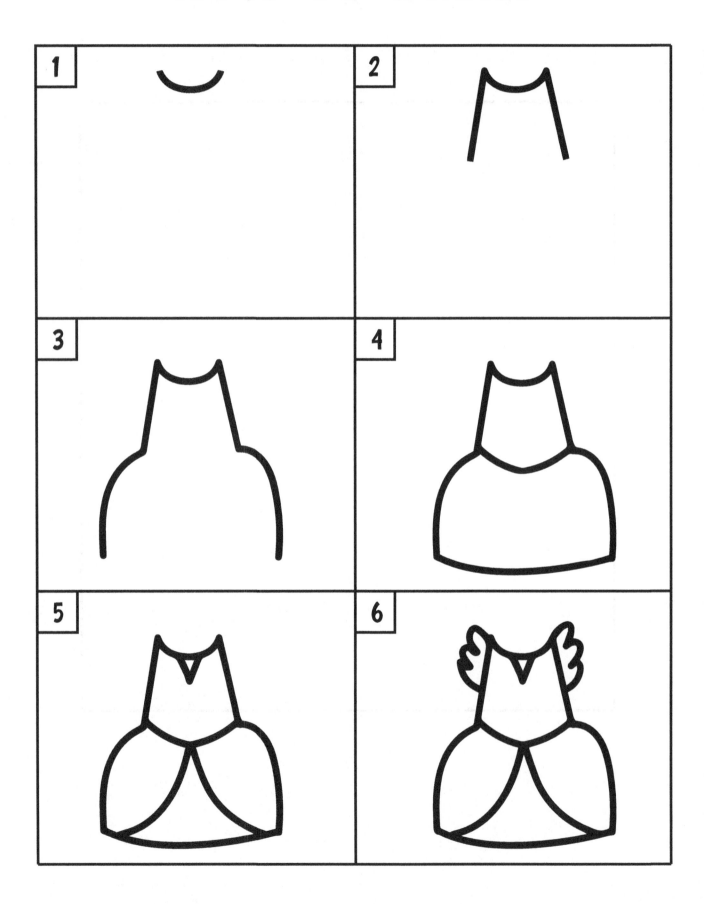

# HOW TO DRAW

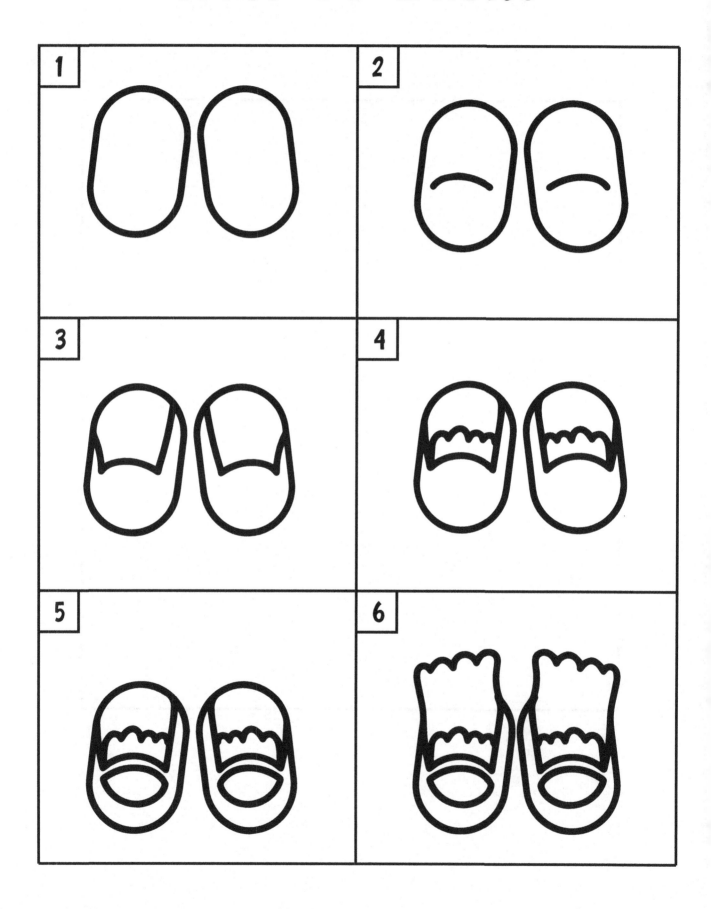

# HOW TO DRAW

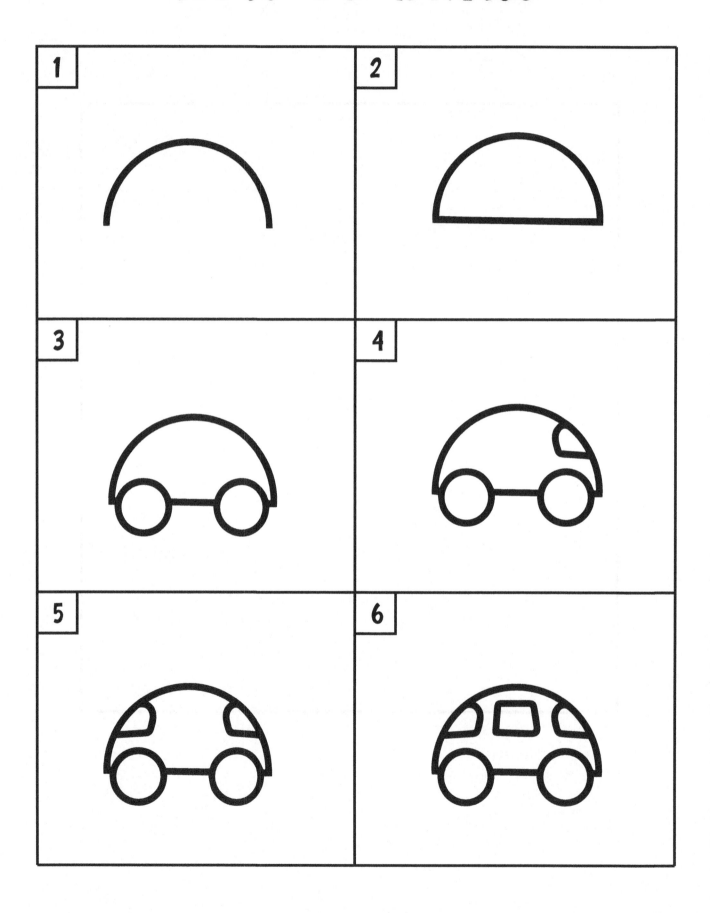

# HOW TO DRAW

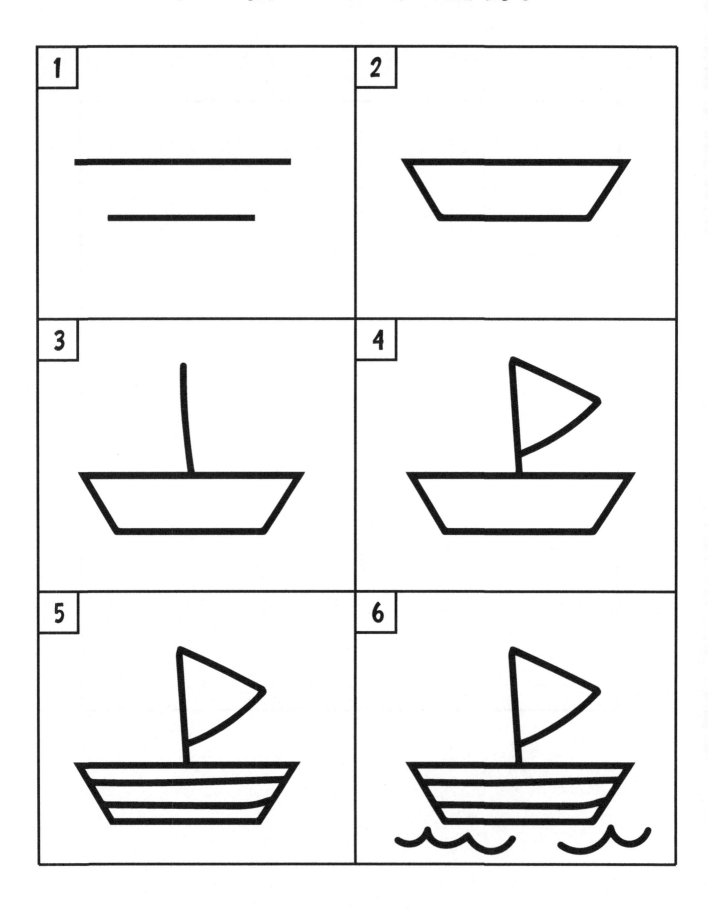

# HOW TO DRAW

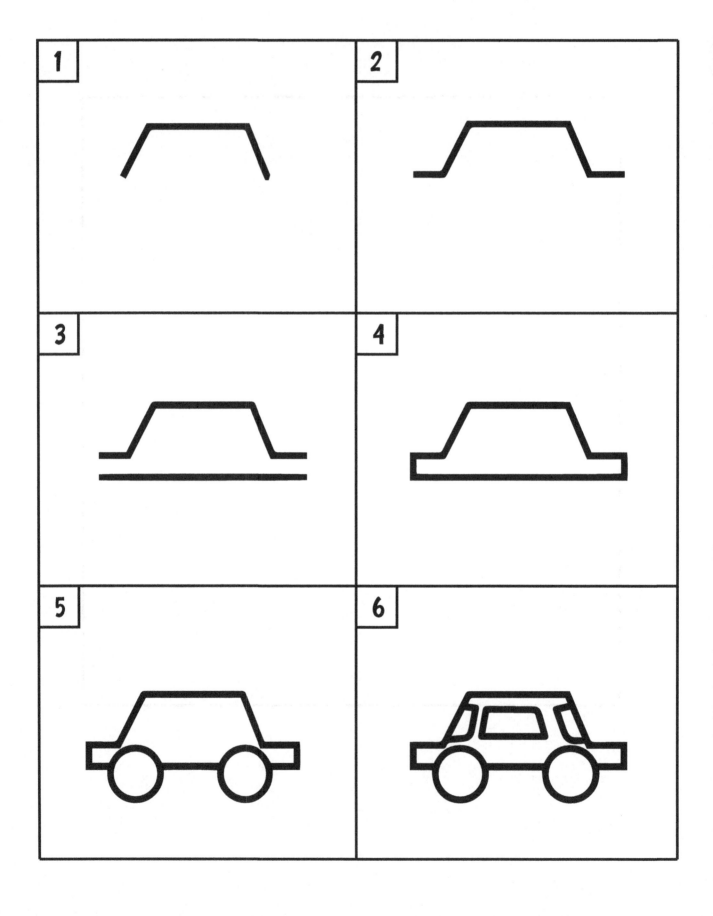

# HOW TO DRAW

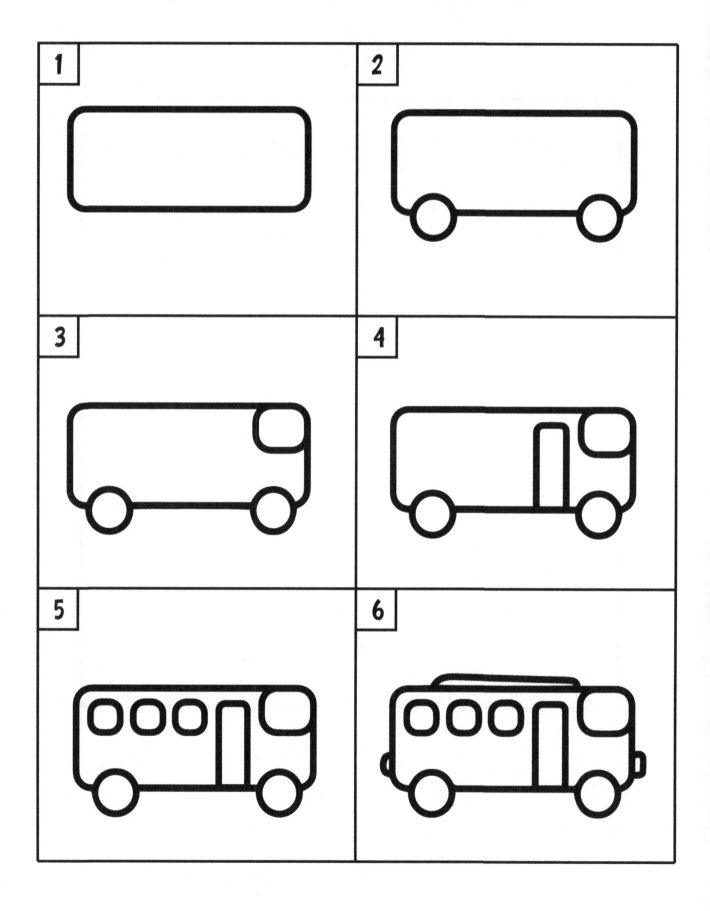

# HOW TO DRAW

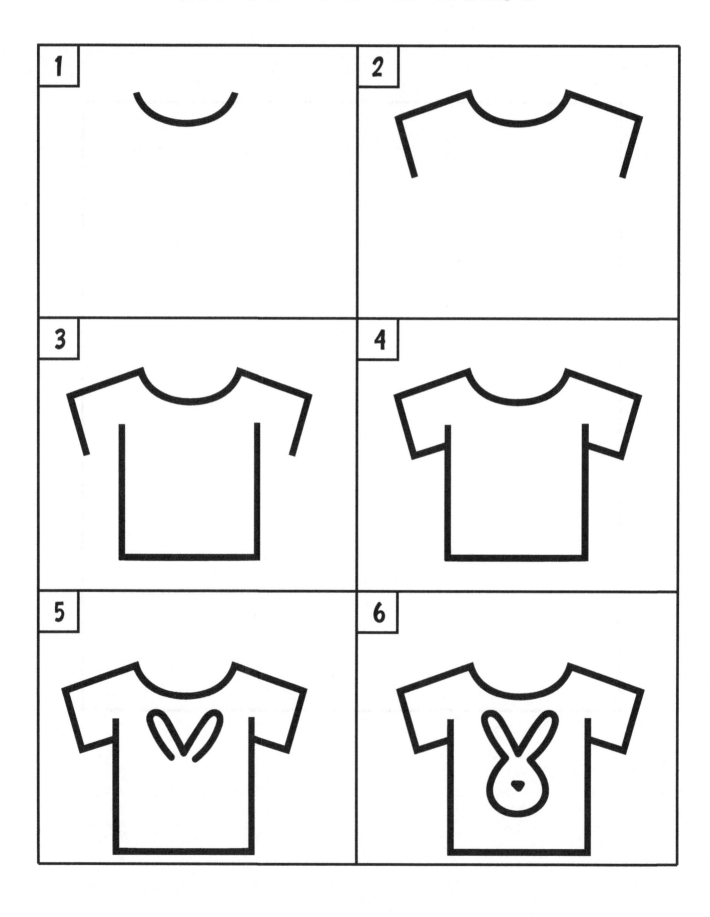

# HOW TO DRAW

# HOW TO DRAW

# HOW TO DRAW

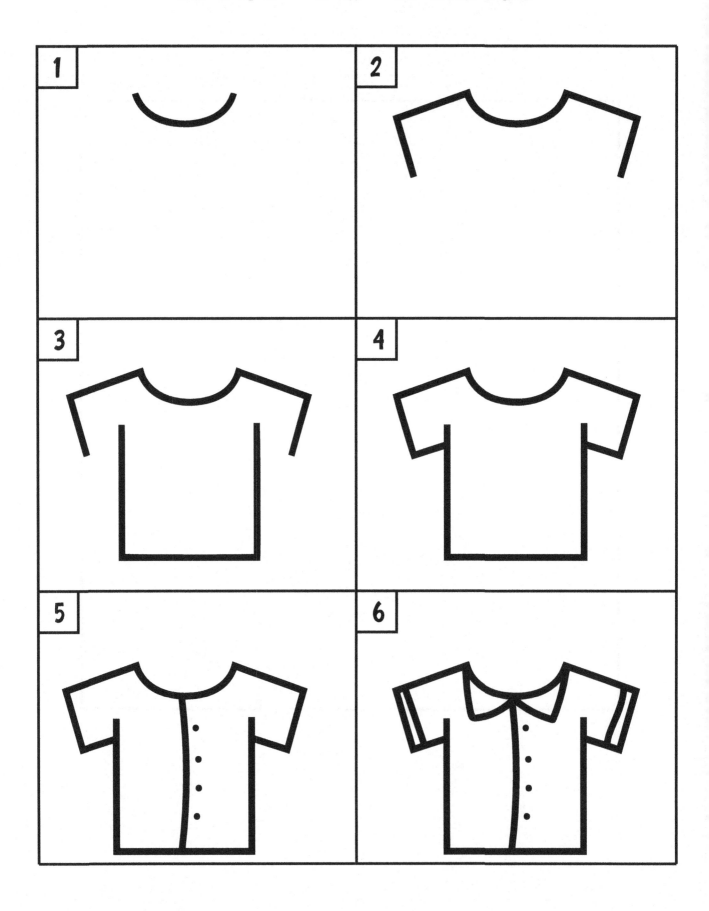

# HOW TO DRAW

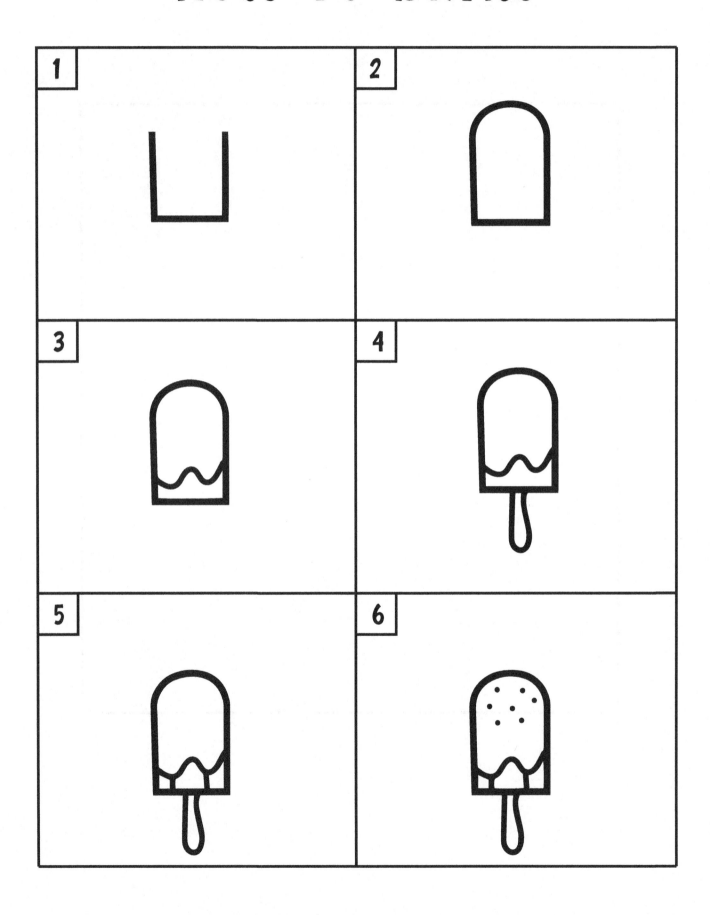

# HOW TO DRAW

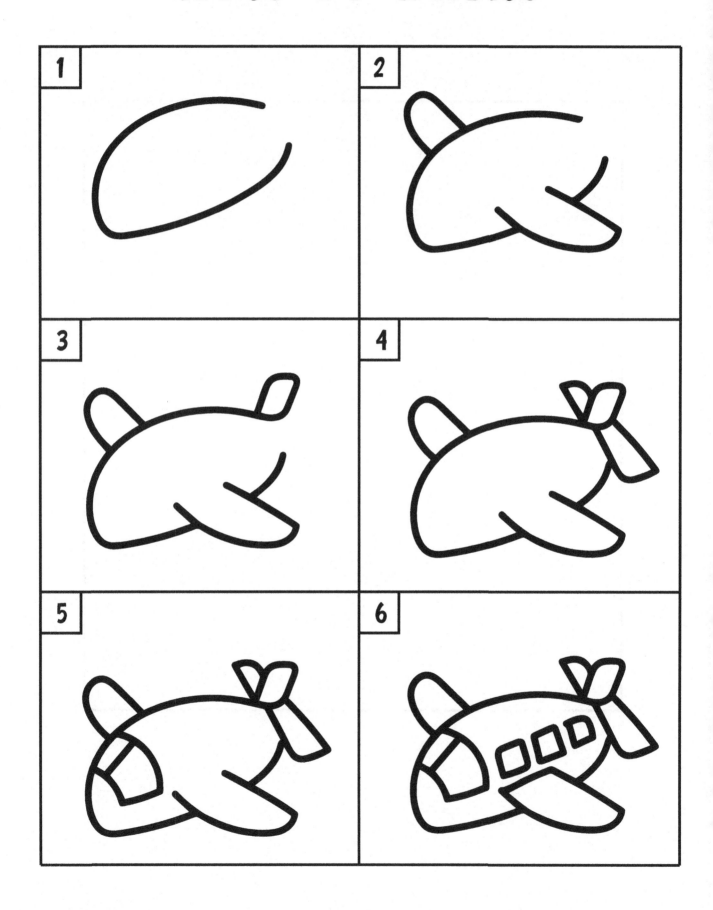

# HOW TO DRAW

# HOW TO DRAW

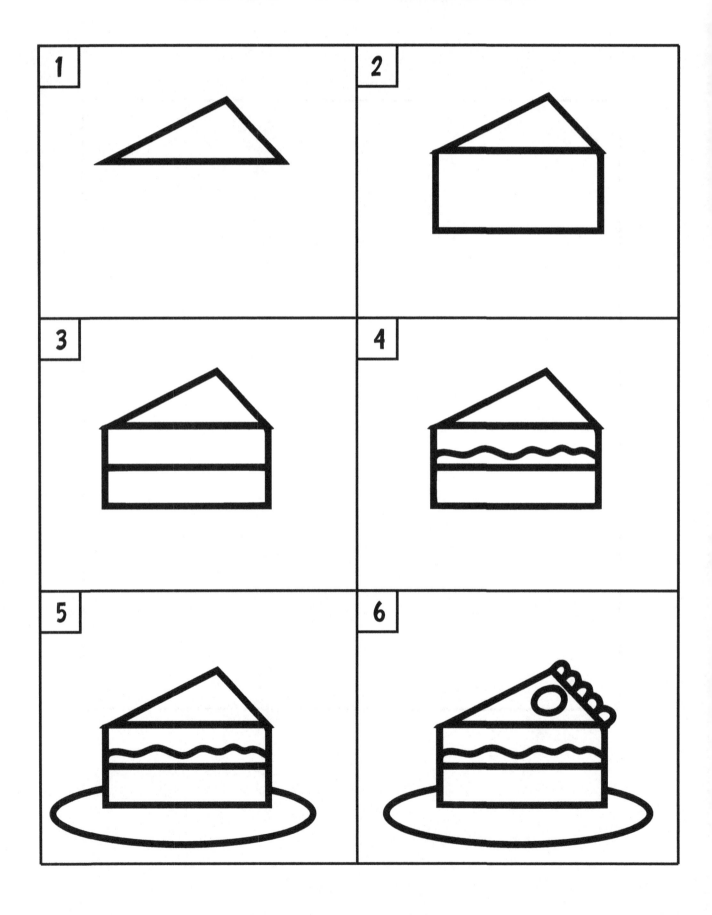

# HOW TO DRAW

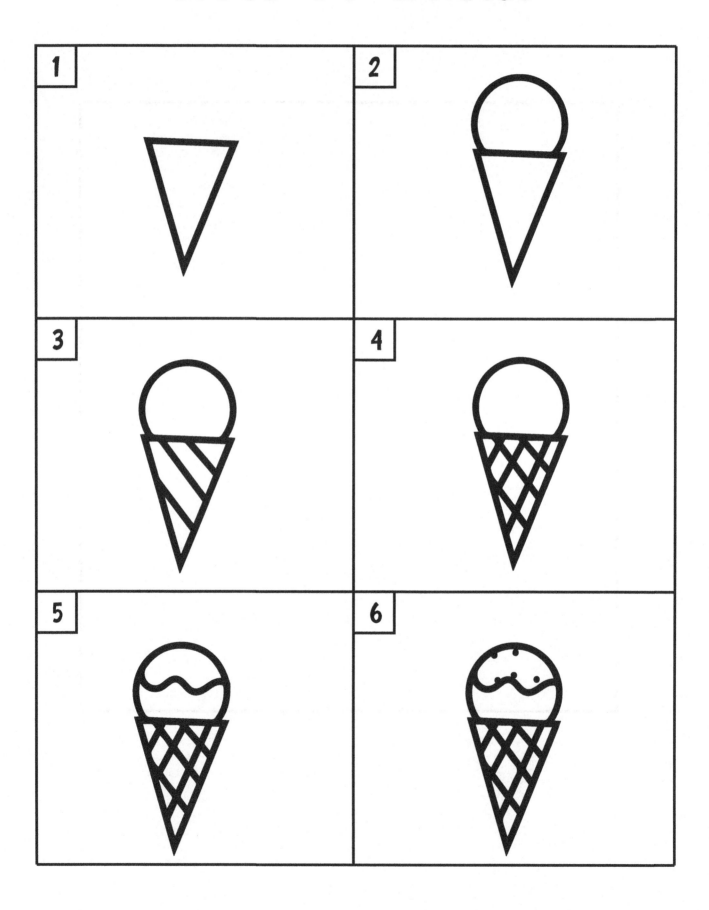

# HOW TO DRAW

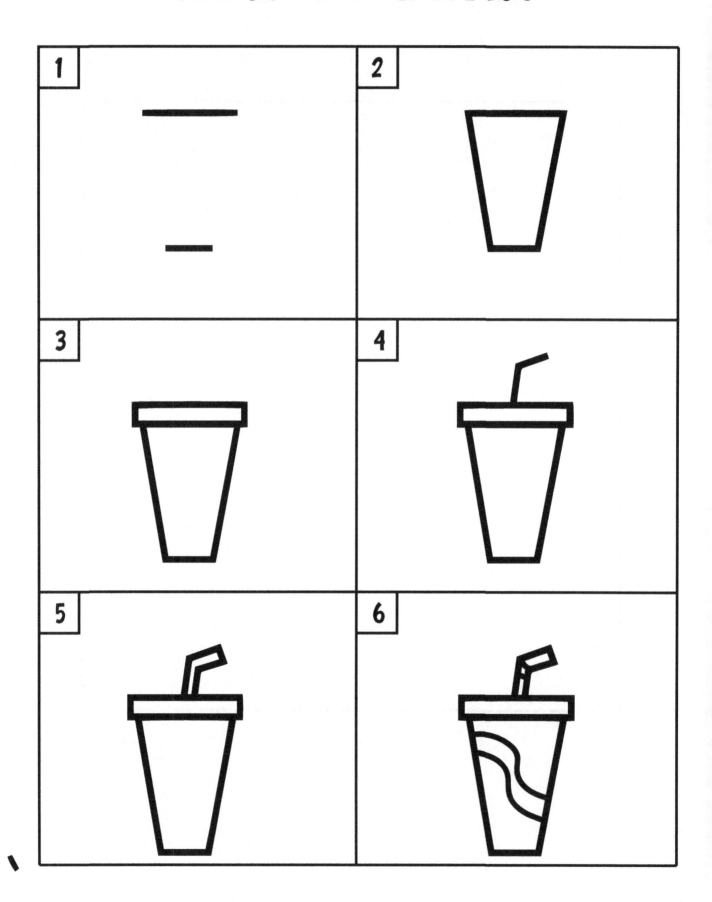

# HOW TO DRAW

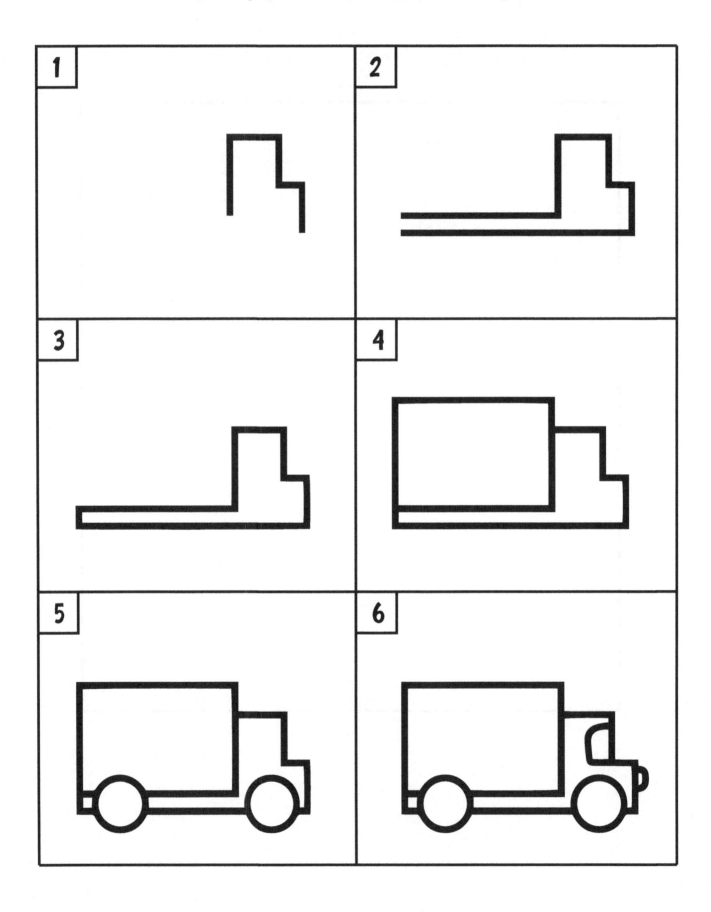

# HOW TO DRAW

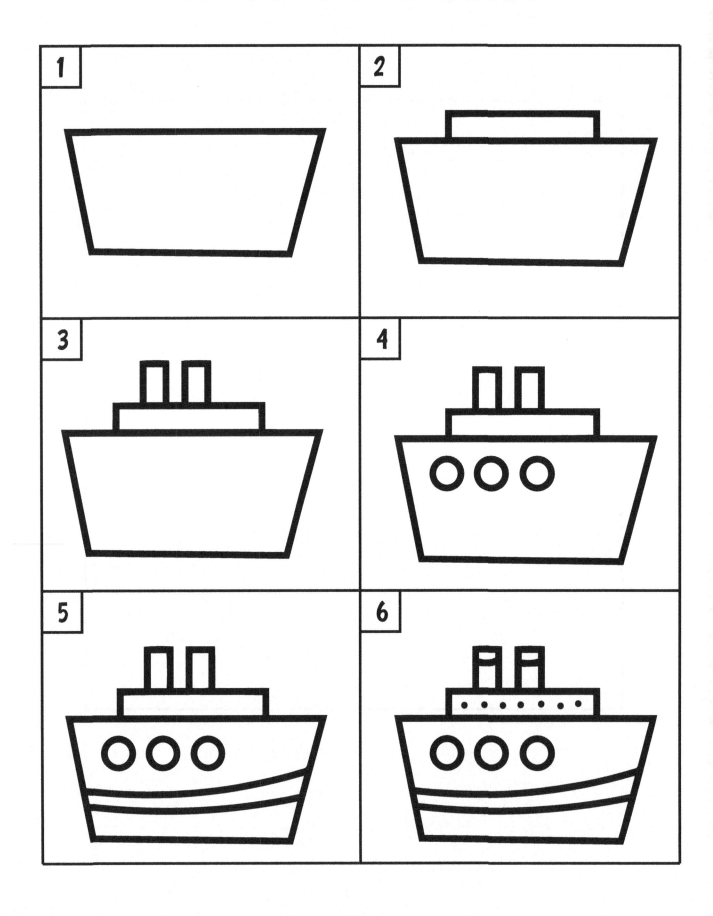

# HOW TO DRAW

# HOW TO DRAW

# HOW TO DRAW

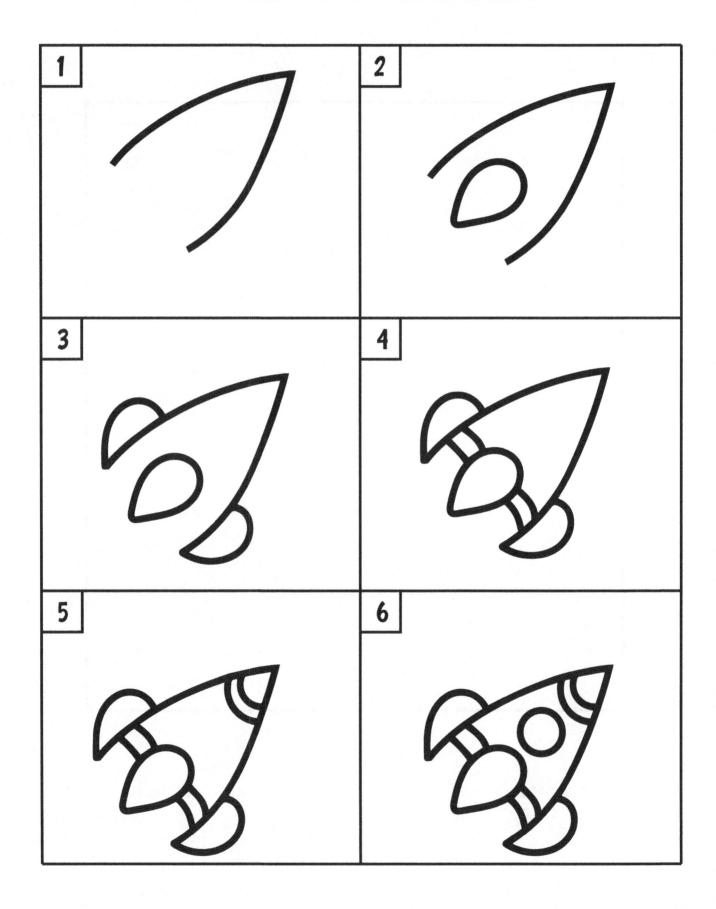

# HOW TO DRAW

# HOW TO DRAW

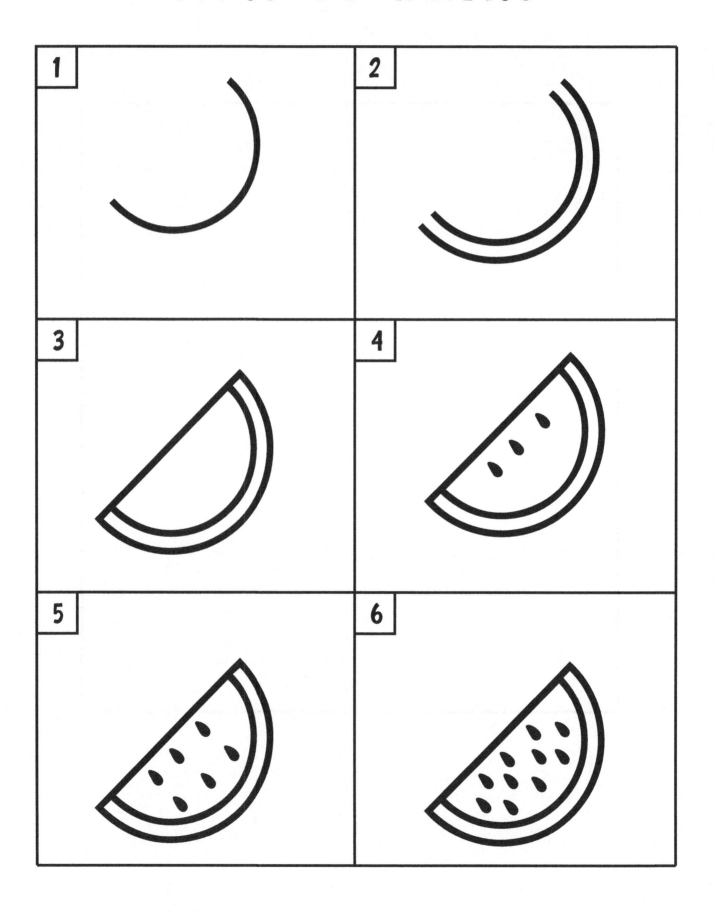

# HOW TO DRAW

# HOW TO DRAW

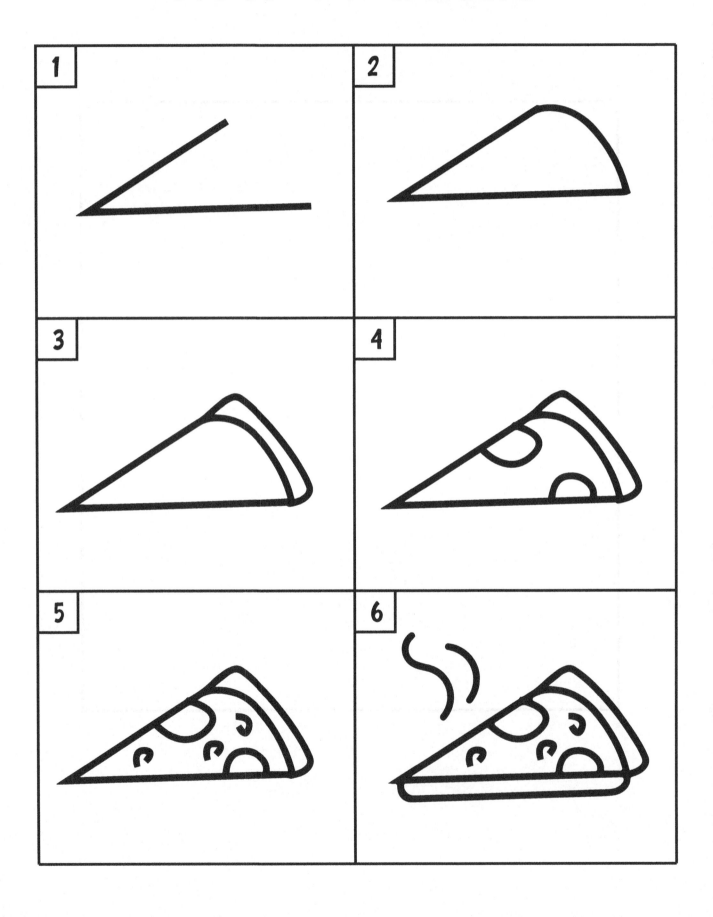

# HOW TO DRAW

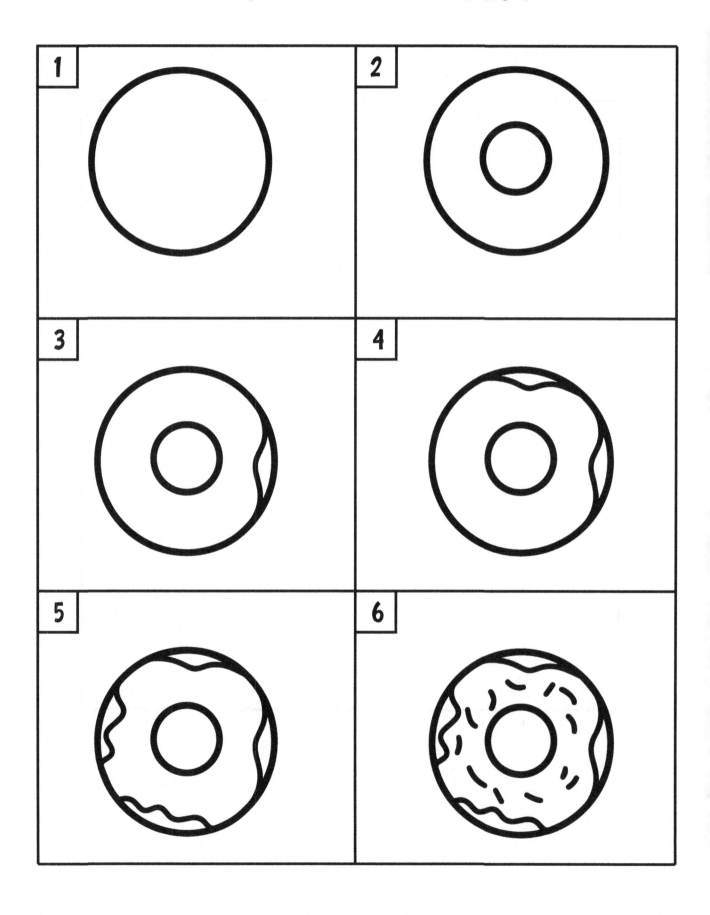

**Thank you for getting our book!**

if you find this drawing book
fun and useful, we would be very grateful
if you post a short review,
it means a lot to us.

Made in the USA
Las Vegas, NV
26 January 2024

84908628R00037